INSECT ATTACK

INSECT ATTACK

CHRISTOPHER LAMPTON

THE MILLBROOK PRESS
BROOKFIELD, CT
A DISASTER! BOOK

Cover photograph courtesy of Photo Researchers © Scott Camazine
Illustrations by Pat Scully
Photographs courtesy of: Superstock: p. 6; Culver Pictures, Inc.: p. 9; Peter Arnold, Inc.: pp. 12, 21 (top), 44, 47, 48–49, 53; Carolina Biological Supply: pp. 16–19, 21 (bottom); Bettmann Archive: p. 23; Photo Researchers: pp. 24 (Gianni Tortoli), 30 (Stephen Dalton), 32–33, 36 (Scott Camazine), 37 (Dan Guravich), 38–39 (Gary Retherford), 42 (Eric V. Grave), 45 (Scott Camazine), 50 (left: Francoise Gohier, right: Stephen Krasemann), 51 (Alan Carey); United Nations: p. 25; New York Public Library, Astor, Lenox and Tilden Foundations: p. 27; U.S. Department of Agriculture: p. 55.

Library of Congress Cataloging-in-Publication Data
Lampton, Christopher.
  Insect attack / Christopher Lampton.
    p.   cm. — (A Disaster! book)
  Includes bibliographical references and index.
  Summary: Introduces various kinds of insects that have wreaked havoc on humanity over the centuries, including locusts, mosquitoes, killer bees, and fruit flies.
  ISBN 1-878841-93-9 (pbk.)
  1. Insect pests—Juvenile literature. [1. Insect pests.]
  I. Title. II. Series: Lampton, Christopher. Disaster! book.
SB931.3.L36 1992
595.7'065—dc20   91-26155 CIP
                                                             AC

Copyright © 1992 by Christopher Lampton
All rights reserved
Printed in the United States of America

123456789 - WO - 96 95 94 93 92

CONTENTS

Invasion of the
Crop Snatchers **7**

Masters of the
Earth **11**

Insect Plagues **22**

Locusts in the
Midwest **26**

Insects Gone
Bad **29**

Disease-Carrying
Insects **41**

Fighting Back **46**

Natural Insect Control **52**

Glossary **57**

Recommended
Reading **59**

Index **61**

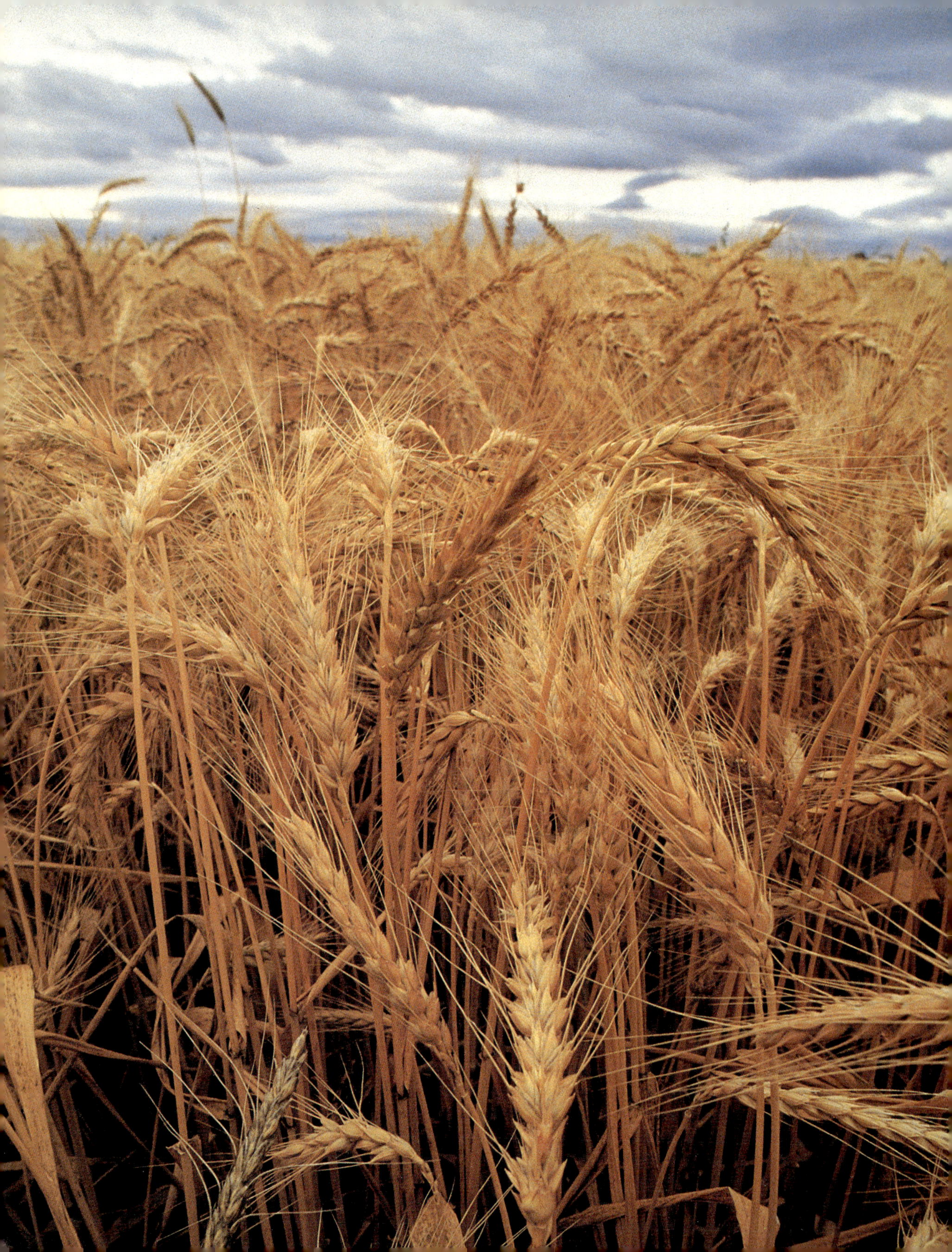

INVASION OF THE CROP SNATCHERS

The year is 1874. You are a young farmer, standing in the doorway of your home, in Kansas. You are right in the middle of that vast stretch of the Midwest known as the Great Plains. Fields of corn, wheat, and other crops stretch before you as far as the eye can see. It is summer, and the air smells fresh and clean. You take a deep breath of that air and think about the big harvest coming up in the fall. At that time, you'll gather up the crops and take them to market to sell.

Suddenly, in the distance, you see what you believe is a storm coming. The sky begins to darken along the horizon, as though

Lush fields of waving wheat have always attracted insect pests.

clouds are gathering. You think about all the chores that need to be done and hope that the storm won't last for very long. You especially hope that it won't be accompanied by tornadoes.

But as the dark cloud moves closer, you realize that it is not an ordinary storm. For one thing, the cloud seems to be making a strange buzzing noise. You've been told that tornadoes sound a little like that, but somehow you know that this is no tornado. In fact, you begin to suspect that it is not even a storm.

Finally, when you can see the cloud up close, you realize that it isn't an ordinary cloud. It is a cloud of insects. Millions, perhaps even billions, of grasshoppers, of a type you've heard people refer to as *locusts,* make up the cloud. They are flying through the air in a giant swarm. As they approach your farm, they swerve downward toward the fields. They cover the corn like a living blanket, attacking each ear as if to devour it whole.

You run shouting in the fields, waving at the insects to chase them away. But the locusts aren't frightened by your shouts. Instead, they start swarming around you. You try to fight them off, but they crawl up your pant legs and down your sleeves. A few even crawl into your mouth, where they leave a bitter taste even after you've spit them out.

You then run back to the farmhouse, where your brothers and sisters help to beat the locusts off your clothing. Fighting nausea, you wash off the grasshoppers that have crawled up your legs and arms. When you are finished, you go to the window to look outside. The locusts are still swarming. There is nothing you can do to stop them.

The locusts remain for two days, eating every bit of food that they can find in your fields. When they finally move on, you have no crops left. The corn has been stripped bare, the wheat scoured

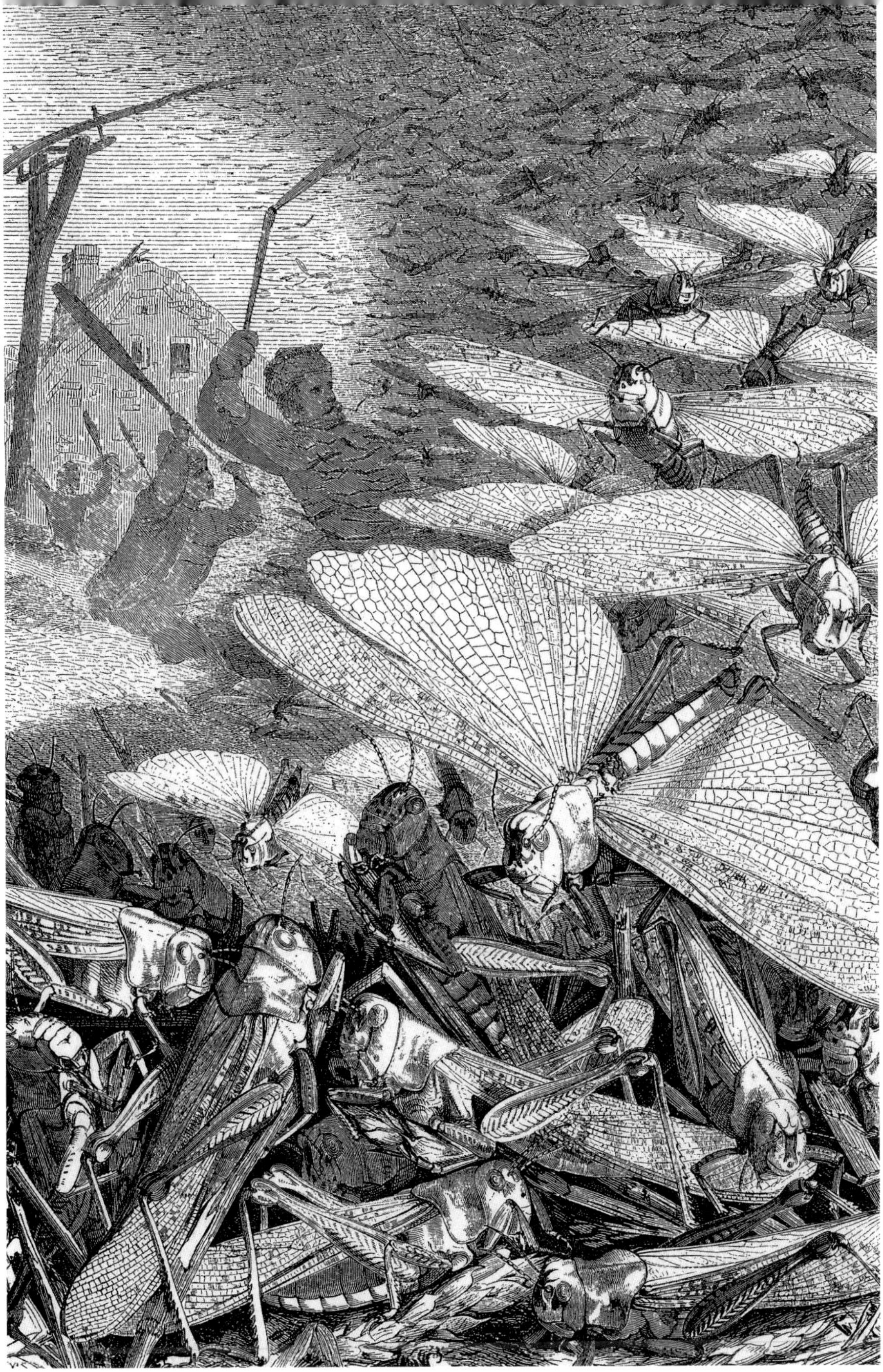

clean. The locusts have even managed to pull up onions from beneath the ground and eat them.

The farm animals stumble about in their pens looking sickly. They eat the dead locust corpses lying on the ground until they start spitting them back up. Somehow you know that the bitterness of the grasshoppers will later make these animals worthless as food.

The coming of the locusts has ended in total disaster. With no crops left, there will be no food for your table—and no income at harvest time. You have no idea how your family will survive the rest of the year.

And there is no way to stop the locusts from returning in years to come.

MASTERS OF THE EARTH

Insects are the most common creatures on earth. They come in over a million different varieties. This is more than all other types of animals combined. They can live just about anywhere, except perhaps in the ocean. (Only one species of insect lives in salt water.)

To biologists—scientists who study living organisms—insects are the most successful creatures around. Human beings like to think that they are the masters of the earth, but the true masters are the insects. They took over long before we got here. They still rule the world today, by sheer force of numbers.

Where do all these insects live? Just look around you. It's possible to fit a lot of insects into a very small space. For instance, about one million insects can live in an open field or section of forest only one acre in size.

Insects, including this red-legged grasshopper, are the most common creatures on earth.

12

But what exactly is an insect? It is an animal belonging to the class of animals known as *insecta.* The *insecta,* in turn, belong to a larger class (or *phylum*) of animals known as the *arthropoda* or *arthropods.* This phylum also includes *arachnids,* such as spiders, and *crustaceans,* such as lobsters and crabs. (If you've ever noticed a resemblance between lobsters and cockroaches, it's because they're distant relatives.)

Nobody would ever claim that all insects look alike. But there is a definite family resemblance between insects. An insect has its

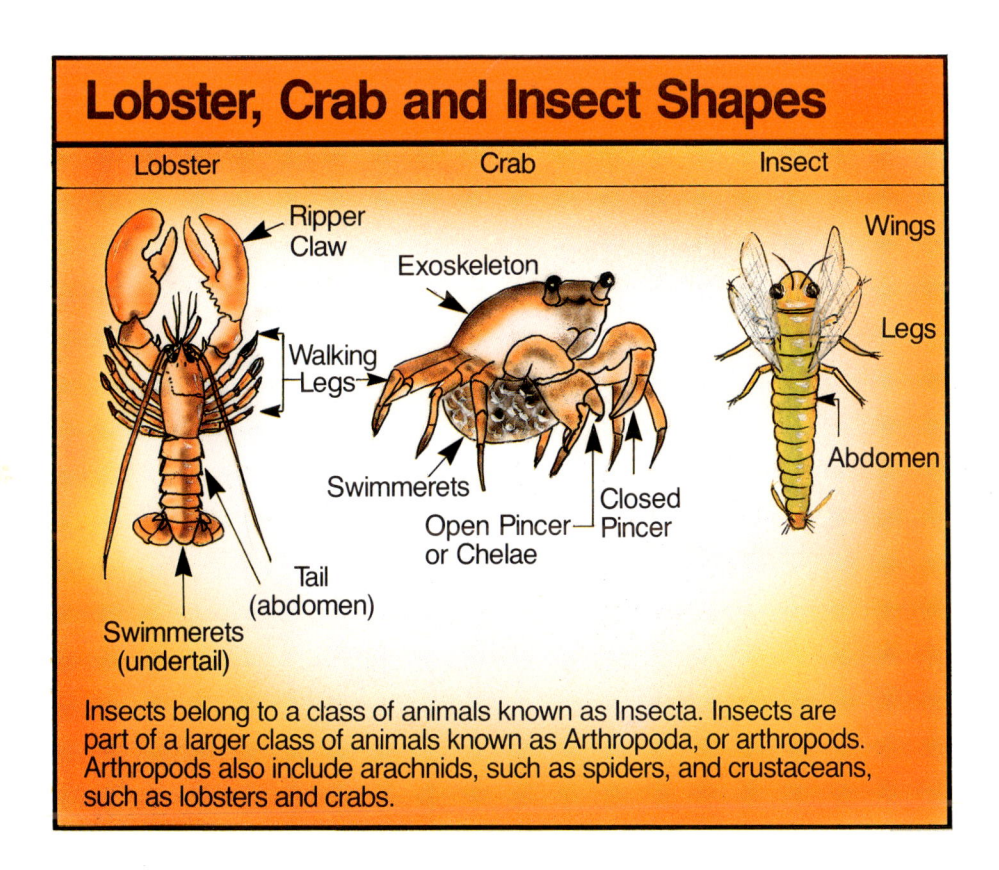

Lobster, Crab and Insect Shapes

Lobster — Ripper Claw, Walking Legs, Tail (abdomen), Swimmerets (undertail)

Crab — Exoskeleton, Swimmerets, Open Pincer or Chelae, Closed Pincer

Insect — Wings, Legs, Abdomen

Insects belong to a class of animals known as Insecta. Insects are part of a larger class of animals known as Arthropoda, or arthropods. Arthropods also include arachnids, such as spiders, and crustaceans, such as lobsters and crabs.

Anatomy of an Insect

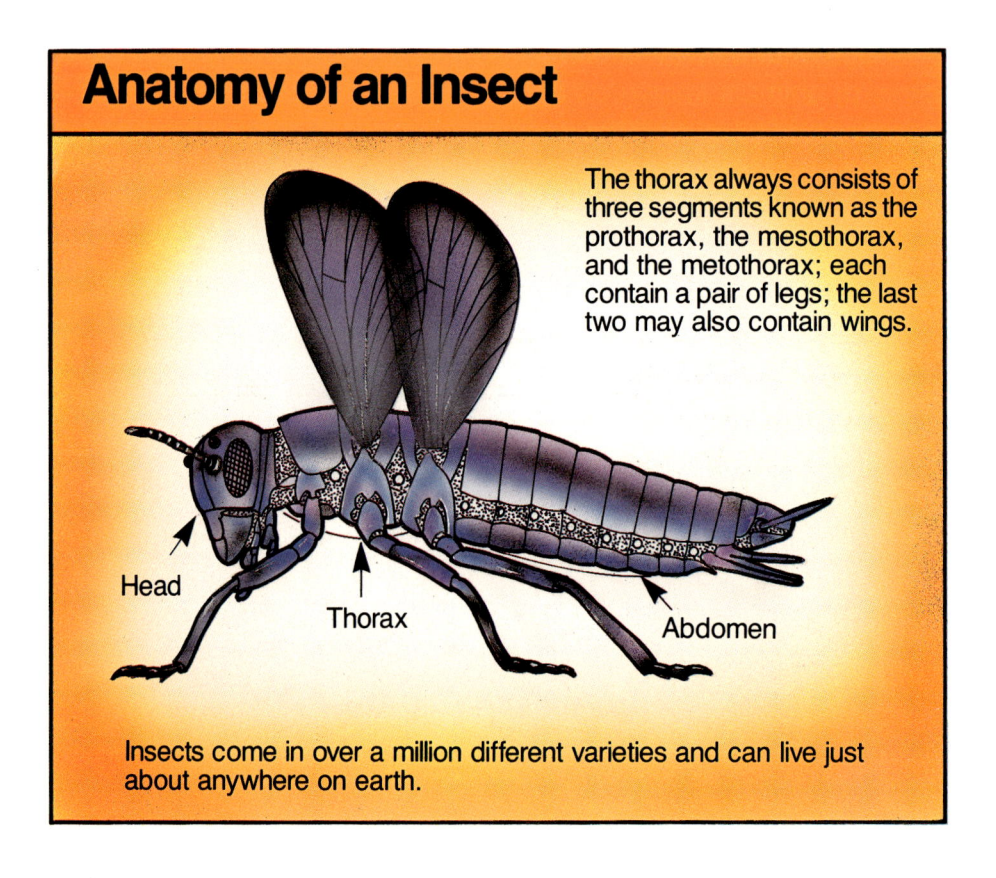

The thorax always consists of three segments known as the prothorax, the mesothorax, and the metothorax; each contain a pair of legs; the last two may also contain wings.

Head

Thorax

Abdomen

Insects come in over a million different varieties and can live just about anywhere on earth.

skeleton (or *exoskeleton*) outside its body. This skeleton is made not of bone but of a hard substance known as *chitin*. An insect's body is divided into segments. The *head* is at the front end, the *abdomen* is at the back end, and the *thorax* is in between. The thorax has three pairs of legs extending from it and usually two sets of wings.

Another important thing that sets insects apart from other animals is their unique life cycle. As they grow up, they pass through a number of distinct stages, actually changing form from one stage to another. This change of form is called *metamorphosis.* Some insects are hatched from eggs, and others are born live. During the first stage of the insect's life, it is called a *nymph, naiad,* or *larva,* depending on the species. These young insects bear no resemblance to the way the insect will look when it becomes an adult. The larvae (plural of larva) are usually soft and wormlike in form. Most insects then go through an adolescent form called a *pupa,* during which they are not even able to move. At the end of the pupal stage, the insect becomes an adult.

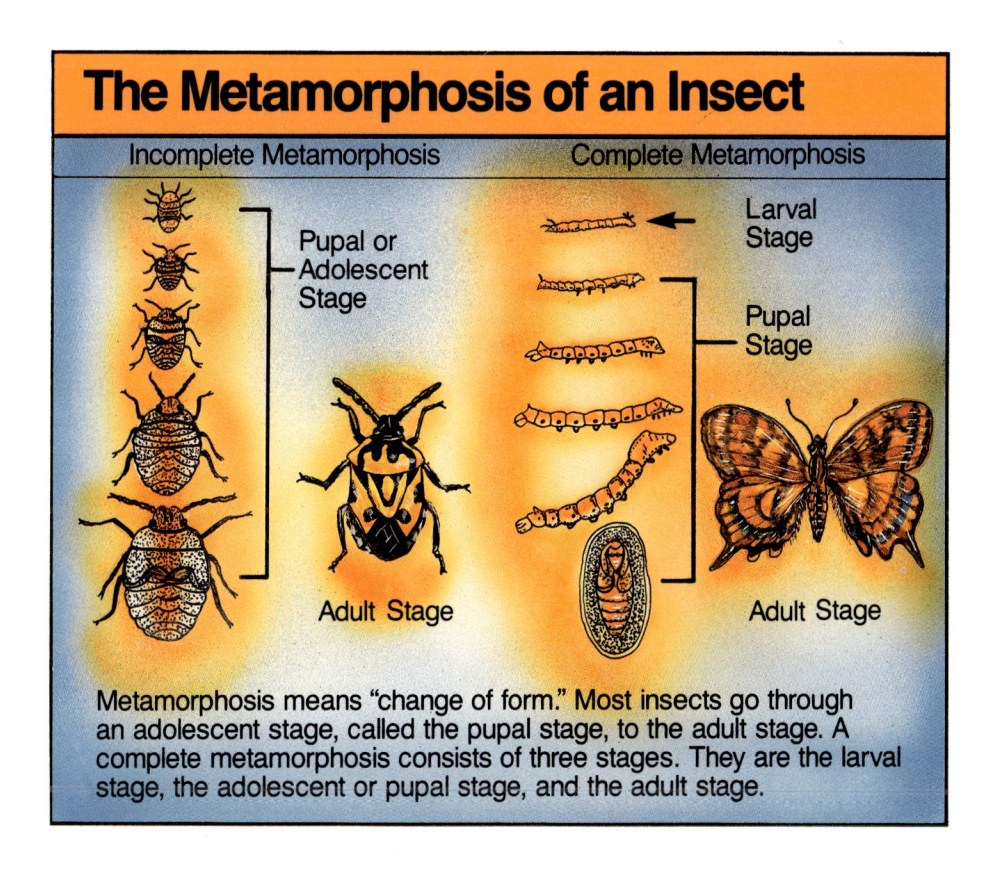

The Metamorphosis of an Insect

Incomplete Metamorphosis

Pupal or Adolescent Stage

Adult Stage

Complete Metamorphosis

Larval Stage

Pupal Stage

Adult Stage

Metamorphosis means "change of form." Most insects go through an adolescent stage, called the pupal stage, to the adult stage. A complete metamorphosis consists of three stages. They are the larval stage, the adolescent or pupal stage, and the adult stage.

Insects that go through all three of these stages are said to go through a "complete" metamorphosis. About 15 percent of insects go through an incomplete metamorphosis, consisting of only some of these stages. A familiar example of a complete metamorphosis is the change of a caterpillar into a butterfly. The caterpillar is the insect's larval stage, and the butterfly is the adult stage. The pupal stage occurs while the creature is inside the familiar white caterpillar "cocoon."

Here and over: this painted lady butterfly can be seen in all its various forms—egg, larva, pupa, and adult.

17

18

19

Common insects include flies, mosquitoes, grasshoppers, beetles, lice, dragonflies, butterflies, ants, wasps, and bees. Spiders and centipedes are *not* insects. Sometimes, however, nonscientists will lump them together with insects into a very nonscientific group of animals called "bugs."

Insects play an important role in keeping our planet running smoothly. For instance, some insects serve as pollinators for plants. Insects such as bees produce food. Other insects are themselves eaten as food by people in some parts of the world.

For the most part, insects and human beings live peacefully together on the planet Earth. But sometimes they come into conflict. For instance, some insects like to eat the same foods that humans do. When insects start devouring crops raised by human farmers, the farmers are understandably upset. Other insects, such as bees and wasps, will attack human beings. Still others can spread disease.

The amount of harm that a single nonpoisonous, non-disease carrying insect can cause to a human being is small. However, insects often travel together in vast swarms. A swarm of insects can be a powerful force of nature, bringing destruction to both crops and people. When large numbers of insects turn aggressive, eating food intended for human beings or attacking humans themselves, the result can be disastrous indeed.

Bees both help with the pollination of plants and produce food—honey— that humans like to eat.

21

INSECT PLAGUES

The destructive power of insects has been noted again and again throughout history. The Bible is filled with references to insect plagues in ancient times. Exodus 10:15, for instance, speaks of a plague of locusts that struck Egypt at the time of Moses: "For they covered the face of the whole earth, so that the land was darkened; and they ate every herb of the land and every fruit of the trees . . . so there remained nothing green on the trees or on the plants of the field throughout all the land of Egypt." That passage is not unlike modern descriptions of the damage caused by locusts.

Swarms of insects can grow to great size because of the speed with which insects multiply. Many female insects, for instance, can lay hundreds or even thousands of eggs at a time—and they can do this several times a year. If there's enough food available to

In this biblical scene, God enables Moses to inflict seven plagues, including pestilence, in ancient Egypt, to free the Jewish people from slavery.

■ 23

support large numbers, and no natural enemies to keep their numbers down, insect populations can grow incredibly fast.

Because swarms of insects can eat large quantities of food, an insect plague is commonly followed by famine. Although insects such as locusts very rarely attack human beings directly, they can often leave starvation in their wake.

Locust plagues have struck in many countries around the world over the centuries. Pictures of locusts appear in ancient Aztec art, as well as on 3,500-year-old Egyptian tombs. One of the worst locust plagues of recent history took place in the United States, a little more than a century ago.

Swarms of insects attacking crops can cause severe famine, especially in poorer countries.

LOCUSTS IN THE MIDWEST

No one knows if there are any Rocky Mountain locusts left on the face of the earth. They may well be extinct. But in the 1870s there were literally billions of them, swarming across the Great Plains states of the American Midwest.

In the summers of 1874 through 1877, swarms of locusts appeared in an area stretching north from Texas to the Dakotas and east from the Rockies to the Mississippi River. A single swarm of Rocky Mountain locusts may have contained as many as 120 billion insects. A typical swarm measured 100 miles wide by 300 miles long. The insects would fly for miles on the wind. Then, whenever the wind let up, they would land and begin devouring all of the food in sight.

Seen from a distance, swarms of locusts looked more like an oncoming storm than a cloud of insects. On landing, they would hit

A cloud of Rocky Mountain locusts darkens the countryside in this artist's depiction of insect attacks on the Great Plains in the 1870s. Farmers fight back using smoke, as cattle flee the scene in terror.

the ground so hard that they would sound, in the words of an eyewitness, "almost like hail."

No food was safe from these insects. They ate whole fields of corn and just about any other kind of vegetable that grew on midwestern farms. They even invaded houses and ate the food off the kitchen tables. Insect corpses piled up in hallways and living rooms, on tables and beds. Animals that ate dead locusts tasted like the locusts when they were cooked. Wells and rivers became choked with millions of dead bugs.

Desperate farmers attempted, in vain, to kill the locusts with smoke and fire. Bulldozer-like devices were called in to forcibly haul away and crush thousands of the locusts at a single swipe.

Over the course of four years, the locusts did more than $200 million worth of damage. They destroyed entire farms and the careers of many farmers. Eventually, the army had to be called in to deliver supplies to the locusts' victims.

Then, in 1877, the locusts began to dwindle in number. By the next year, they had almost completely vanished.

Since the turn of the century, no Rocky Mountain locusts have been seen in the United States or elsewhere. What happened to them? No one knows. But there is a chance that they still exist—and may even return in another locust plague.

A similar invasion hit the Great Plains in the twentieth century. During the great drought of the 1930s, dry conditions turned the American Midwest into a so-called Dust Bowl. At that time, a plague of hungry grasshoppers descended on the fields of farmers already hard hit by dry conditions that had lasted for several years.

INSECTS GONE BAD

Of the more than one million species of insect that populate this planet, the vast majority live in peaceful harmony with the human race. Only a few insect species cause problems. Here's a look at some of these:

■ **LOCUSTS** Locusts are a type of grasshopper. They come in two forms, called "phases": the *solitary phase* and the *gregarious phase*. As the names imply, solitary locusts like to be alone, and gregarious locusts like to travel in large swarms.

Locusts have the unusual ability to change into either of these two different forms depending on how large the current locust population happens to be. If the current population is small, most of the locusts will be solitary. But if the population starts growing, most of the locusts will switch into the gregarious phase. The locusts' phys-

Locusts can take one of two forms, the gregarious phase (left) and the solitary phase, depending on current environmental conditions.

ical form actually changes. They grow larger and turn new colors. They take on different feeding and mating habits. They grow longer wings so that they can fly for greater distances. Then they begin to travel from place to place in large swarms.

A swarm of gregarious locusts can be a deadly natural force. As they travel, the locusts need to eat. Like busy commuters, they eat and run. And they lay eggs as they go, preparing the way for new swarms of locusts to be born the next year.

■ **KILLER BEES** Reporters and scientists had been warning the citizens of the United States for years. The so-called killer bees were on their way here. Then, in 1990, the invading insects finally arrived. But just what are killer bees? And should you be worried about them?

Killer bees are the accidental creation of Dr. Warwick Kerr, a German-American scientist living in Brazil. In 1956, Dr. Kerr flew to Africa to study African honeybees. He observed that African honeybees produced much more honey than the European bees normally found in the Americas. Unfortunately, the African bees were also much more aggressive and likely to sting people than were European bees. He shipped a cargo of the bees to Brazil, where he attempted to breed them with European bees. He hoped to develop a hybrid bee—a bee with the desirable characteristics of both African and European bees. The hybrid, he hoped, would produce more honey but would not be aggressive.

Unfortunately, some of the African bees escaped. They soon bred with European bees, but their offspring were just as aggressive as the pure African kind. These fierce hybrid bees are technically called *Africanized bees.* They have become known to the public as killer bees, however, because they more readily attack human beings than do the familiar European kind.

In the 1970s, reports began to appear of Brazilians being attacked and killed by large swarms of these bees. For instance, in his book *Killer Bees,* author and television reporter Anthony Potter tells the story of Domingos Massucheto. A sixty-five-year-old Brazilian farmer, Massucheto was attacked in 1973 by a large swarm of killer bees that lived on the roof of his house. One afternoon, for no known reason, the bees attacked Massucheto's two horses. Then they turned on his dog. When the farmer tried to help the dog, they attacked him. Witnesses say that Massucheto was covered by a swarm of bees as thick as a blanket. They stung him hundreds of times, until he died from heart failure. Although Massucheto was known to have a heart condition, the bee venom clearly contributed to his death. At the autopsy, 80 bees were found in Massucheto's stomach. He had apparently swallowed them while screaming.

Many other such stories appeared in the press during the 1970s. But while the bees were terrorizing Brazilians, they were making their way slowly north, toward the United States. News reports suggested that the bees would arrive by the end of the 1980s. U.S. citizens were told to prepare for an onslaught of bees more vicious than any seen in this country before.

A swarm of Africanized bees in Mexico.

In 1990, researchers for the U.S. government captured the first invading killer bees, near the Texas border. They were traced to a hive containing a colony of 5,000 Africanized bees.

Should you start preparing for the day when these bees move into your neighborhood? Not necessarily. Some scientists believe that the killer bees won't be all that much worse than the bees that are already here. The same precautions that you've probably been taking all your life around normal bees will also apply to killer bees.

European Honeybee/Africanized Bee

European Honeybee | Africanized Bee

The European honeybee bred with the African bee produces the fierce hybrid known as the Africanized bee.

Bees are most dangerous to those who are allergic to bee stings. If you've been stung by bees in the past and have suffered an allergic reaction, then you should try to stay away from areas where bees are commonly found. If you are stung, seek medical help immediately. If you've never been stung and don't know whether you are allergic, it's best to seek medical assistance if you are stung, just to be safe.

It has been estimated that, when killer bees have spread throughout most of the United States, there will be roughly 100 deaths each year from bee stings. This may sound like a large number. But there are already 40 deaths in this country each year from bee stings, so this is not really a huge change.

The sting of an Africanized bee is exactly the same as that of a European bee. The only difference is that the Africanized bee is more likely to sting. Thus, if you're stung by an Africanized bee, there's no reason to panic (though you might want to shout and jump up and down a few times, until the pain passes). The important thing is to keep your distance from the hives of Africanized bees. In large numbers, Africanized bees are definitely more dangerous than European bees.

■ **FRUIT FLIES** Fruit flies certainly aren't as flashy as killer bees, but they are indeed a menace to farmers around the world. This is because they lay their eggs in fruit. Apple maggots, for instance, lay their eggs in apples and plums. These eggs then hatch into larvae. As they grow, the young fly larvae feed on the fruit to keep themselves alive. A single larva can eat its way through an entire piece of fruit, destroying any value that the fruit might have had.

In 1980 and 1981, the state of California suffered a devastating infestation. The Mediterranean fruit fly, known popularly as the "medfly," lives in citrus fruits. It probably entered California in an imported load of fruit, though there are strict laws that are supposed to prevent infested fruit from entering the state.

At first, the authorities tried to control the medflies by releasing sterile male medflies into the environment. These flies were specially treated so that they could not father offspring. But to no avail. Eventually, the infestation was brought under control with the aid of a pesticide called malathion.

The Mediterranean fruit fly, which can devastate citrus crops.

A young boll weevil worm in a cotton boll.

■ **WEEVILS** Weevils are a kind of beetle, often no larger than a quarter of an inch in size. Like fruit flies, many species of weevil lay their eggs in growing plants to provide the young with food. As the insect matures, the plant is damaged and sometimes destroyed.

The best-known weevil in the United States is the cotton boll weevil (or just "boll weevil," for short). It was given this name because it places its eggs in the bolls, or seedpods, of the cotton plant. Cotton was at one time the main crop of the American South, and an infestation of boll weevils could destroy an entire field of growing plants.

Other types of weevil include the granary weevil, which can destroy stored grain, and the rice weevil, which can similarly destroy stored rice. Still other weevils damage fruits and nuts, hay, corn—even the tips of pine branches.

■ **ANTS** Ants may be the most familiar of all insects. We find them crawling on our lawns, our sidewalks, even our kitchen tables. They are small and seemingly harmless, though anyone who has ever been bitten by one knows that even a single ant can cause pain. And if a single ant can cause pain, imagine what an entire colony of ants can do!

A migrating colony of army ants in the Costa Rican rain forest.

Ants rarely act alone. In some ways, we can think of a colony of ants as a single organism—a single, *large* organism. A colony of ants acting as a single organism can do a lot of damage indeed, especially when it comes time to eat. Fortunately, most of the more vicious species of ants live close to the equator, away from the more heavily populated countries of the temperate zones.

Army ants, for instance, have been known to migrate in large numbers, much like locusts. These ants are carnivorous (meat-eating) and will attempt to consume any creature, living or dead, that lies in their path. This mostly means other insects, but birds, lizards, and snakes are also frequent victims, and so is the occasional large animal. A swarm of army ants can be as much as 40 feet wide and consist of tens of thousands of individual ants.

Driver ants engage in similar migrations and are even more voracious. A famous 1847 report on them claims that these ants will attack pigs, birds, and monkeys. However, a well-known modern ant expert named Edward O. Wilson suggests that the terrors of the driver ant are greatly exaggerated, that these ants aren't really that dangerous. Why? Because they move so slowly that even the most sluggish larger animals can generally get out of their path before they can do much damage.

DISEASE-CARRYING INSECTS

Some insects carry diseases. Usually, the diseases are caused not by the insects themselves but by tiny organisms that live in the insects' bodies. Insects such as fleas, mosquitoes, and ticks live by sucking blood from other animals, including human beings. When an insect bites someone, the organisms it carries are transferred to the person that was bitten, and that person may come down with the disease.

One of the most devastating diseases of the Middle Ages was the *bubonic plague.* The so-called Black Death struck Europe in the middle of the fourteenth century. More than 20 million people—almost half the total population—were killed by the disease before it was over.

The tiny organism that causes bubonic plague is known as *Yersinia pestis.* It is often carried by fleas. Ordinarily, these fleas

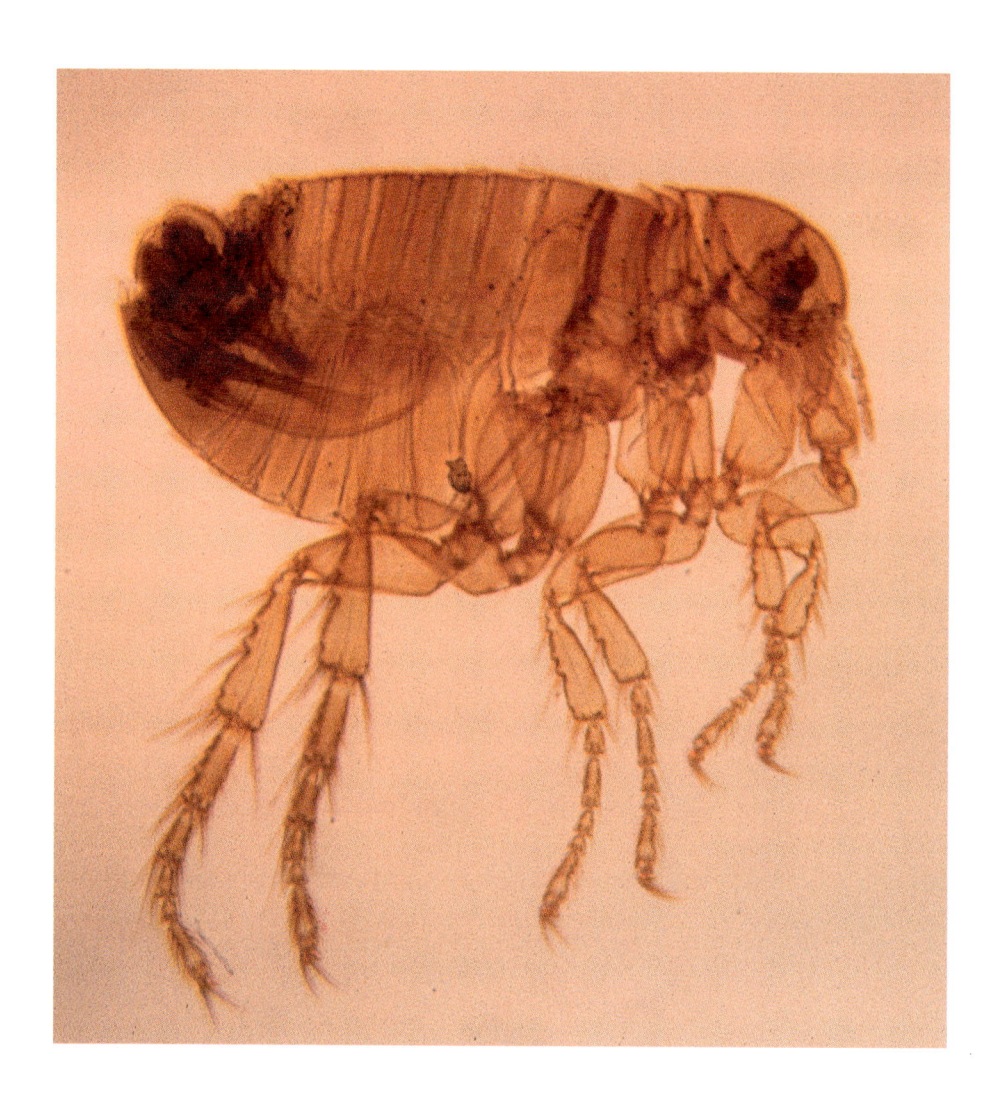

Fleas can often transmit serious illness. Living on the bodies of rats, dogs, cats, and even humans, they can pass on tiny infectious organisms they are harboring.

live on the bodies of small animals, such as rats, and don't bother human beings. But if large numbers of the small animals that the fleas normally live on die off, they will find larger animals to infest, such as humans. These humans can contract bubonic plague. They will then spread the disease to other human beings without the help of fleas. Epidemics of bubonic plague have frequently occurred after attempts were made to exterminate (kill off) rats.

Another deadly disease carried by insects is *malaria* (Italian for "bad air"). This disease is commonly found in countries near the equator. Malaria is caused by tiny organisms known as *protozoa,* which are frequently carried by mosquitoes. When a mosquito bites a victim, the protozoa enter that person's blood. There they begin to multiply, making the person quite ill.

One of the greatest weapons against malaria has been the chemical *DDT.* DDT can kill great numbers of mosquitoes. We'll have more to say about DDT and other *insecticides* in the next section.

Lyme disease is a debilitating disease spread by ticks. It was first discovered in Lyme, Connecticut, and it has spread across New England and into other nearby areas. Many other diseases are also spread by insect *vectors,* a term that scientists use to describe the agent that carries disease germs from one individual to another.

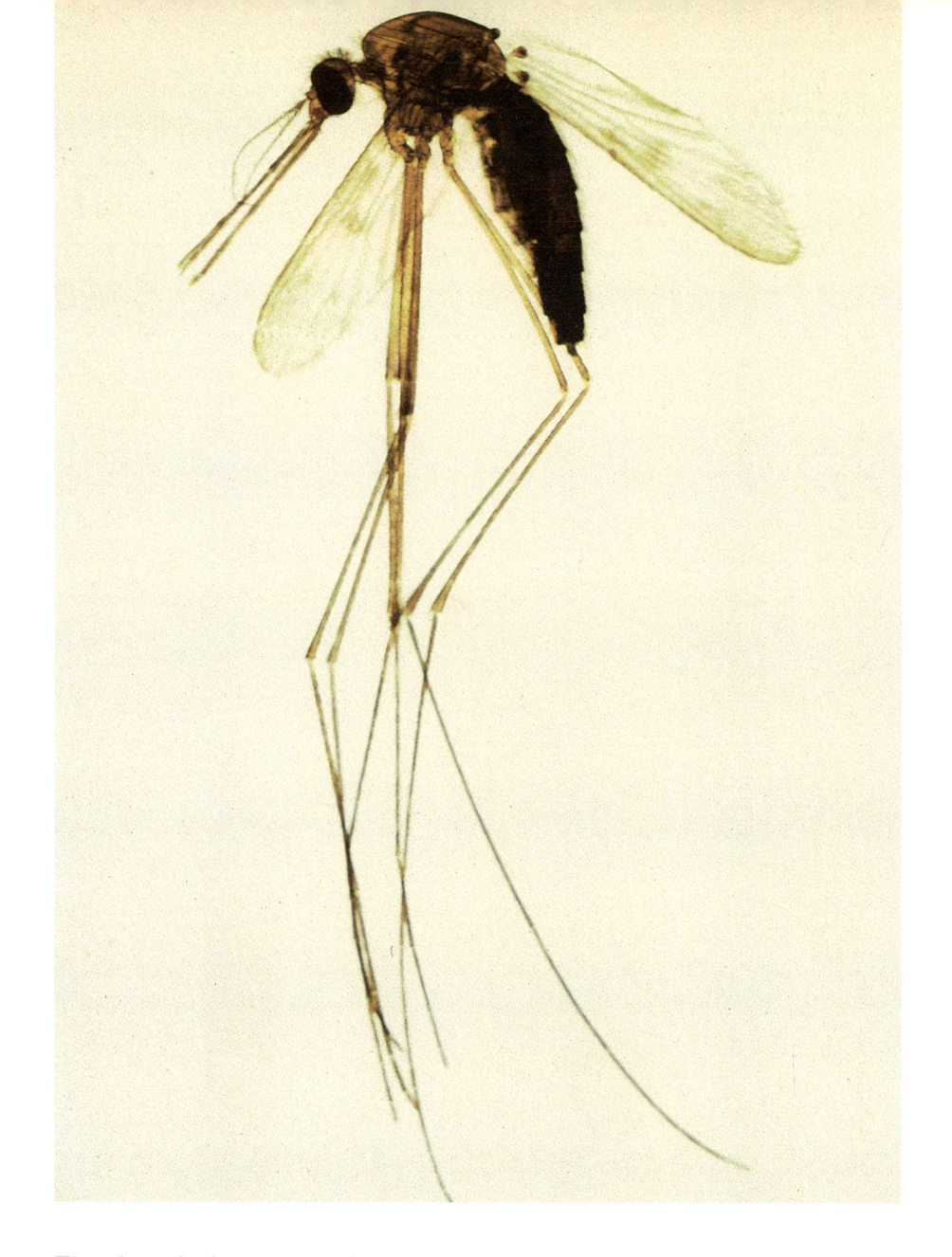

The Anopheles *mosquito, carrier of malaria.*

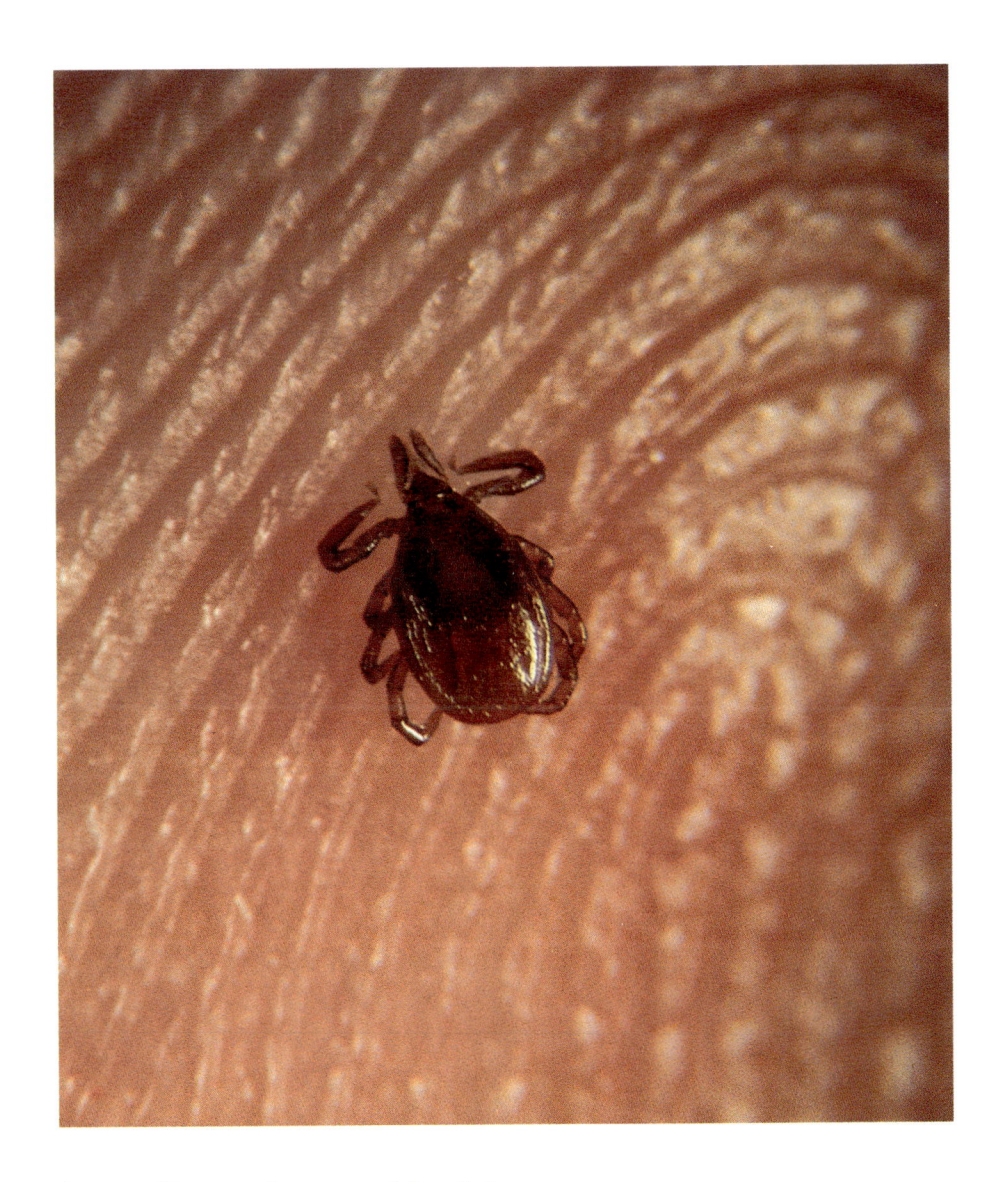

*Lyme disease is spread by ticks,
such as this one, that bite humans.*

FIGHTING BACK

People have been fighting insects for a long time. More than two thousand years ago, the Romans boiled asphalt to produce foul fumes that would chase away insects. The ancient Egyptians used similar techniques more than a thousand years before the Romans.

Insecticides—insect-killing substances—are nothing new. However, a wide range of these insect poisons were developed by scientists in the nineteenth and early twentieth centuries. The insecticides were made out of metallic compounds. Metallic compounds are chemicals that contain metals, such as mercury, lead, arsenic, potassium, and iron. Unfortunately, these insecticides were not only poisonous to insects, they were poisonous to human beings and other animals as well. Because insects are relatively small, it is possible to poison them with very tiny doses of these chemicals, doses

A plane spraying California crops with a pesticide.

too tiny to harm humans. But the insecticides, when applied to plants, would seep into the soil. There they could build up to deadly levels.

Just before World War II, a new group of insecticides was created. These new insecticides were made from organic compounds, or chemicals based on the element carbon. Although they are also poisonous, organic compounds tend to decay over time in the same way that plants do. In theory, this should prevent them from building up to poisonous levels in the soil. The best known of the organic insecticides, invented in 1939, is dichlorodiphenyltrichloroethane, also known as DDT.

The ladybug is a beneficial insect that kills off other insect pests. Insecticides often kill off the "good bugs" along with the "bad ones."

Insecticides have proven to be a great help to farmers, who once lost large portions of their crops to insect pests. In addition, they have helped greatly in fighting diseases spread by insects.

But they have their drawbacks. Some critics of their use argue that insecticidal poisons are sometimes absorbed by the very crops that they are intended to protect. Thus, they may poison people who eat food that is sprayed with them. In addition, farm workers exposed to insecticides over an extended period may become ill as a result of this exposure. And insecticides can kill beneficial insects, such as bees, as well as pests.

Some insecticides, such as DDT, can find their way into the *food chain.* This means they are absorbed by plants or small organisms that are in turn eaten by animals. These animals may, in turn, be eaten by still other animals. Each animal that eats food contaminated with DDT itself becomes contaminated with DDT. Many birds that eat food contaminated with DDT lay eggs that crack before the young birds are ready to be born. Several species of birds have come close to extinction due to DDT poisoning.

For these and other reasons, many insecticides are now banned in the United States and in other countries. However, food contaminated with these insecticides can still be imported into the United States from countries where they are not banned.

The brown pelican (left), bald eagle (right), and osprey (above) are all endangered, due partly to the use of pesticides, which have poisoned their habitat.

NATURAL INSECT CONTROL

Because of the problems caused by insecticides, many farmers are beginning to use methods of insect control that don't involve poisons. For instance, crops can be planted at a time of year when insect populations are low. Predators can be used to kill and devour the insects before their populations can grow. Some scientists have even tried to breed new crops that are naturally insect resistant. Unfortunately, none of these methods alone is effective with the vast majority of insect pests.

Somewhat more effective are insect hormones. These are chemicals produced by the insects themselves that cause them to undergo certain physical changes. For instance, some hormones will interfere with insect reproductive cycles. If pests are sprayed with large quantities of these hormones, their populations will eventually begin to dwindle.

Bats such as this one are important insect predators.

Finally, certain viruses and bacteria may prove themselves quite useful for insect control. Sprayed on insect populations, these can kill a specific type of insect and leave the rest of the environment unharmed.

In an ideal world, human beings wouldn't need to kill insects. There would be enough food in the world for the insect populations and humans alike.

Unfortunately, there are millions, perhaps even billions, of people around the world on the verge of starvation. If we are to avoid famine and mass suffering, we must protect our food supply from insects. However, in the war against insect *depredators*—a word sometimes used for insects that attack human beings and their food supply—we must recognize that insects have a right to live on our planet, too.

In an ideal world, insects and humans would live side by side in peace. But the reality is that there are millions of people dying from starvation, and insects contribute to this by devastating crops.

55

GLOSSARY

abdomen—the rear section of an insect's body.
Africanized bees—hybrid African-European bees; sometimes called killer bees, because they are more aggressive than unhybridized European bees.
arachnids—the class of animals that includes spiders; distant relatives of insects.
arthropoda—the phylum of animals to which insects belong.
bubonic plague—an epidemic disease that has devastated Europe on several occasions, most notably in the fourteenth-century epidemic known as the Black Death; bubonic plague is commonly spread by fleas.
chitin—the hard substance from which an insect's exoskeleton is made.
crustaceans—the class of distant relatives of the insects that includes lobsters and crabs.
DDT (dichlorodiphenyltrichloroethane)—the best-known organic insecticide, created in 1939.
depredators—literally, "plunderers"; a term sometimes used to describe insects that devastate crops.

exoskeleton—the hard outer covering on an insect's body, made of chitin.
food chain—the sequence in which food energy passes from one living organism to another.
gregarious phase—the phase in which locusts swarm with other locusts.
head—the front section of an insect's body.
insect—an animal distinguished by a body divided into three segments (head, thorax, and abdomen) and by a hard outer covering known as an exoskeleton; a member of the class *insecta*.
insecta—the class of animals known popularly as insects.
insecticides—poisonous substances designed to kill insects.
larva—a newborn insect.
locust—a variety of grasshopper known for its voracious, and sometimes destructive, appetite.
Lyme disease—a disease spread by ticks; first discovered in Lyme, Connecticut.
malaria—a disease commonly found in countries near the equator; malaria (from Italian words meaning "bad air") is spread by mosquitoes.
metamorphosis—the process by which insects change from larvae (plural of larva) to pupae (plural of pupa) to adults.
phylum—a scientific division used to group related types of living organisms together.
protozoa—tiny organisms that can cause disease; often carried by mosquitoes.
pupa—an adolescent insect, usually immobile, changing from the larval form to the adult form.
solitary phase—the phase, or physical form, in which a locust does not swarm with other locusts.
thorax—the middle section of an insect's body, with three pairs of legs and usually two pairs of wings.
vector—anything that carries disease-causing germs from one animal to another, such as mosquitoes and other insects that spread diseases.

RECOMMENDED READING

Callahan, Philip S. *Insects and How They Function.* New York: Holiday House, 1971.

Cole, Joanna. *An Insect's Body.* New York: William Morrow & Co., 1984.

Dallinger, Jane. *Grasshoppers.* Minneapolis: Lerner Publications, 1981.

Goor, Ron and Nancy. *Insect Metamorphosis: From Egg to Adult.* New York: Atheneum, 1990.

Pringle, Laurence. *Here Come the Killer Bees.* New York: William Morrow & Co., 1986.

Suzuki, David. *Looking at Insects.* New York: Warner, 1987.

INDEX

Page numbers shown in *italics* refer to illustrations.

Abdomen, 14
Adult, 15, 16, *19*
Africanized bees, 31-35, *32-33,* 34
Animals, 10, 28, 31, 40, *42,* 43, 50
Anopheles mosquitoes, *44*
Ants, 20, *38,* 38-40, *39*
Apple maggots, 35
Arachnids, 13
Army ants, *38-39,* 40
Arsenic, 46
Arthropods, 13, *13*
Aztec Indians, 24

Bacteria, 54
Bald eagles, *50, 51*
Bats, *53*
Bees, 20, *21,* 31-35, *32, 33,* 49
Beetles, 20, 37
Bible, the, 22, *23*
Biologists, 11
Birds, 40, *50,* 50-51, *51*
Black Death, 41
Boll weevils, 37, *37*
Brazil, 31-33
Brown pelicans, *50, 51*
Bubonic plague, 41, 43
Bugs, 20
Butterflies, 16, *16-19,* 20

Caterpillars, 16
Centipedes, 20
Chitin, 14
Citrus fruits, 36, *36*
Cockroaches, 13
Cocoon, 16
Corn, 7, 8, 28, 37
Cotton boll weevils, 37, *37*
Crabs, 13
Crops, *6,* 7, 8, 10, 20, *24, 25, 36, 47,* 49, 52, *55*
Crustaceans, 13

DDT (dichlorodiphenyltrichloro-ethane), 43, 48, 50-51
Depredators, 54
Disease-carrying insects, 20, 41, *42,* 43, *44, 45,* 49
Dragonflies, 20
Driver ants, 40
Dust Bowl, 28

Eggs, 15, *16,* 22, 30, 35, 37, 50-51
Egypt, 22, *23,* 24
Epidemics, 41, 43
Exodus, 22

Famine, 24, *25*
Fighting insects, 46, *47,* 48–51, *48–51*
Fleas, 41, *42,* 43
Flies, 20
Food chain, 50
Fruit flies, 35-36, *36*
Fruits, 35-37, *36*

Grain, 37
Granary weevils, 37
Grasshoppers, 8, 10, *12,* 20, 29 (*see also* Locusts)
Great Plains insect attacks, 7, 8, 10, 26, *27,* 28
Gregarious phase of locusts, 29-30, *30*

Hay, 37
Head, 14
Honey, *21*
Hormones, insect, 52

Insect attacks
    ants, 40
    biblical, 22, *23*
    Brazil (1973), 31-32
    Great Plains, 7, 8, 10, 26, *27,* 28
    killer bees, 31-32
    locusts, 7, 8, 10, 22, 24, 26, *27,* 28, 30
Insecticides, 36, 43, 46, *47, 48-51,* 48-52
Insects
    attacks by (*see* Insect attacks)
    body parts of, 14, *14*
    definition of, 13
    disease-carrying, 20, 41, *42,* 43, *44, 45,* 49
    fighting, 46, *47,* 48-51, *48-51*
    as food producers, 20, *21*
    as food source, 20
    life cycle of, 14-16, *16-19*
    natural control, 52, *53,* 54

■ 62

Insects (*continued*)
    plagues of, 7, 8, 10, 22, *23,* 24, 26, *27,* 28
    as plant pollinators, 20, *21*
    problem causing, 29-40
    reproduction and, 15, 22, 24, 30, 35-37, 52
    swarms of (*see* Swarms)
Iron, 46

Kerr, Warwick, 31
Killer bees, 31-35, *32, 33*
Killer Bees (Potter), 31

Ladybugs, *48-49*
Larva, 15, 16, *17*
Lead, 46
Legs, 14
Lice, 20
Life cycle of insects, 14-16, *16-19*
Lizards, 40
Lobsters, 13
Locusts, 8, 10, 22, 24, *24,* 26, *27,* 28-30, *30*
Lyme disease, 43, *45*

Malaria, 43, *44*
Malathion, 36
Massucheto, Domingos, 31-32
Mediterranean fruit fly ("medfly"), 35-36, *36*
Mercury, 46
Metallic compounds, 46
Metamorphosis, 15-16, *15-19*
Monkeys, 40

Moses, 22, *23*
Mosquitoes, 20, 41, 43, *44*

Naiad, 15, 16, *17*
Natural control of insects, 52, *53,* 54
Nuts, 37
Nymph, 15, 16, *17*

Onions, 10
Organic compounds, 48
Ospreys, *50, 51*

Pesticides, 36, 43, 46, *47, 48-51,* 48-52
Phases of locusts, 29-30, *30*
Pigs, 40
Plagues of insects, 7, 8, 10, 22, *23,* 24, *24, 25,* 26, *27,* 28
Plants, 37, 48, 50
Potassium, 46
Potter, Anthony, 31
Predators, 52, *53*
Problem causing insects, 29-40, *32, 33, 36-39*
Protozoa, 43
Pupa, 15, 16, *18*

Rats, 43
Red-legged grasshoppers, *12*
Reproduction of insects, 15, 22, 24, 30, 35-37, 52
Rice, 37
Rice weevils, 37
Rivers, 28
Rocky Mountain locusts, 26, *27,* 28

Skeleton (exoskeleton), 14
Snakes, 40
Solitary phase of locusts, 29, *30*
Spiders, 13, 20
Swarms, 20
    of ants, 40
    of killer bees, 31-32, *32, 33*
    of locusts, 7, 8, 10, 22, 24, *24,*
        26, *27,* 28, 30

Thorax, 14
Ticks, 41, 43, *45*

United States
    Great Plains insect attacks, 7, 8,
        10, 26, *27,* 28

United States (*continued*)
    insecticides and, 51
    killer bees and, 31, 33-35

Vectors, 43
Vegetables, 28
Viruses, 54

Wasps, 20
Weevils, 37, *37*
Wells, 28
Wheat, *6,* 7, 8
Wilson, Edward O., 40
Wings, 14, 30

Yersinia pestis, 41